Anonymous

Exercises at the Ceremony of Unveiling the Statue of John Marshall

Chief justice of the United States, in front of the Capitol, Washington, May 10, 1884. With the address of Mr. Chief Justice Waite, and the oration of William Henry Rawle. Vol. 1

Anonymous

Exercises at the Ceremony of Unveiling the Statue of John Marshall
Chief justice of the United States, in front of the Capitol, Washington, May 10,
1884. With the address of Mr. Chief Justice Waite, and the oration of William Henry
Rawle. Vol. 1

ISBN/EAN: 9783337149451

Printed in Europe, USA, Canada, Australia, Japan

Cover: Foto ©ninafisch / pixelio.de

More available books at **www.hansebooks.com**

EXERCISES AT THE CEREMONY

OF

UNVEILING THE STATUE

OF

JOHN MARSHALL,

CHIEF JUSTICE OF THE UNITED STATES,

IN FRONT OF

THE CAPITOL, WASHINGTON,

MAY 10, 1884.

With the Address of Mr. CHIEF JUSTICE WAITE, and the
Oration of WILLIAM HENRY RAWLE, Esq., LL.D.

WITH THE PROCEEDINGS OF THE PHILADELPHIA BAR RELATING
TO THE MONUMENT TO CHIEF JUSTICE MARSHALL.

———————

WASHINGTON:
GOVERNMENT PRINTING OFFICE.
1884.

AN ACT to authorize the erection of a statue of Chief Justice MARSHALL.

Be it enacted by the Senate and House of Representatives of the United States of America in Congress assembled, That the President of the Senate and the Speaker of the House of Representatives do appoint a joint committee of three Senators and three Representatives, with authority to contract for and erect a statue to the memory of Chief Justice JOHN MARSHALL, formerly of the Supreme Court of the United States; that said statue shall be placed in a suitable public reservation, to be designated by said joint committee, in the city of Washington; and for said purpose the sum of twenty thousand dollars, or so much thereof as may be necessary, is hereby appropriated out of any money in the Treasury not otherwise appropriated.

Approved March 10, 1882.

CEREMONIES

CHIEF JUSTICE MARSHALL

In pursuance of the foregoing act of Congress the Joint Committee on the Library in connection with the trustees of the Marshall Memorial Fund, contracted with and have received from the artist W. W. Story, a bronze statue of John Marshall, late Chief Justice of the United States.

It has been placed on the site selected near the west front of the Capitol.

In accordance with separate resolutions of the two houses, the statue was on the tenth of May, 1884, unveiled in the presence of both houses of Congress, the chief officers of the various Departments of the

Government, the descendants of Chief Justice MARSHALL, and many citizens, with appropriate ceremonies, as follows:

Order of exercises at the unveiling of the statue of John Marshall, late Chief Justice of the United States.

ON SATURDAY, MAY 10, 1884. ✓

MUSIC.

Marine Band.

PRAYER - - - - - *Rev. Dr. Armstrong.*

MUSIC.

ADDRESS - - - - - - - - *The Chief Justice.*

MUSIC.

ORATION - - *William Henry Rawle, Esq.*

MUSIC.

BENEDICTION.

By direction of the Joint Committee on the Library, Hon. John Sherman, chairman, introduced the Chief Justice of the Supreme Court of the United States as presiding officer.

The Rev. Dr. J. G. Armstrong, pastor of the Monumental Church, Richmond, Va., then delivered the following prayer:

O God—Father, Son, and Holy Spirit! We adore Thee as the Father of all mankind, and of our Lord Jesus Christ, the centre and bond of the great brotherhood of man, in whom there is neither Jew nor Greek. We adore Thee as the answerer of prayer, who holdest in Thy grasp all the physical, intellectual, political, and moral forces of the world, and canst adjust and direct them to intelligent and beneficent ends. In this faith we pray to-day for Thy blessing upon our nation in all her governmental departments. Direct her

legislators, in Congress and State legislatures, to the enactment of such laws as
shall secure to all the people of the land
their full constitutional rights, and as shall
be in conformity to that higher law whose
seat is the bosom of God, and whose
voice the harmony of the world. May her
judges, supreme and subordinate, interpret
the laws under the lights of strict integrity
and justice. And in the hands of her
executives may the laws be administered
irrespective of party or sectional interest,
without partiality and without hypocrisy.

And we bless Thy name for all that Thou
hast done for our nation. We bless Thee
for her great men, for her warriors, her
statesmen, her orators, her poets, and her
men of science, come they from whatever
quarter — North, South, East, or West —
who have been such powerful factors in the
production of the national character and
reputation. And especially do we to-day

bless Thee for the life of him whose statue is now to be unveiled, whom a nation honors, and whose memory a nation would cherish and perpetuate. May the example of his pure personal and juridic life stimulate the private citizen and the ermined judge to the faithful performance of duty and the emulation of his great virtues. And may Thy kingdom come and Thy will be done as in heaven so in our land, and so in all the earth, through Jesus Christ our Lord, who liveth and reigneth with the Father and the Holy Spirit, ever One God, world without end. Amen.

Hon. Morrison R. Waite, Chief Justice of the United States, spoke as follows:

ADDRESS

BY

CHIEF JUSTICE WAITE.

Chief Justice MARSHALL died in Philadelphia on the 6th of July, 1835. The next day the bar of that city met and resolved "that it be recommended to the bar of the United States to co-operate in erecting a monument to his memory at some suitable place in the city of Washington." The committee charged with the duty of carrying this recommendation into effect were Mr. Duponceau, Mr. Binney, Mr. Sergeant, Mr. Chauncey, and Mr. J. R. Ingersoll. A few days later the bar of the city of New York appointed Mr. S. P. Staples, Mr. R. M. Blatchford, Mr. Beverley Robinson, Mr. Hugh Maxwell, and Mr. George Griffin to represent them in the work which had thus been inaugurated. Undoubtedly there were similar organizations in other localities, but the publications of the day, to which access has been had, contain no notice of them. The Philadelphia committee, "desiring to make the subscriptions as extensive as possible, and to avoid inconvenience to those who may be willing to unite with them," expressed the wish "that individual subscriptions should be moderate, and that the required amount may be made up by the number of contributions, rather than the magnitude of particular donations, so that the monument may truly be the work of the bar of the United States, and an enduring evidence of their veneration for the memory of the illustrious deceased." Accordingly, in Philadelphia no more than ten dollars was received from any one member, and the committees of other localities were advised of the adoption of this regulation. In this way the sum of three thousand dollars was collected, and then the subscriptions stopped. Not so, however, the work of the Philadelphia committee—or, as I prefer to call them, the Philadelphia trustees—for a few years ago the last survivor of them brought out their package of securities, and it was shown that under their careful and judicious management the $3,000 of 1835 had grown in 1880 to be almost $20,000.

At this time it was thought something might be done by the bar alone to carry out, in an appropriate way, the original design; but Congress, in order that the nation might join the bar in honoring the memory of the great man to whom so much was due, added another $20,000 to the lawyers' fund, and to-day Congress as well as the bar has asked you here to witness the unveiling of a monument which has been erected under these circumstances.

For twenty-four years there sat with the Chief Justice on the bench of the Supreme Court one whose name is largely associated with his own in the judicial history of the times. I need hardly say I refer to Mr. Justice Story. Fortunately a son of his, once a lawyer himself, had won distinction in the world of art, and so it was specially fit that he should be employed, as he was, to develop in bronze the form of one he had from his earliest childhood been taught to love and to revere. How faithfully and how appropriately he has performed his task you will soon be permitted to see.

But, before this is done, let me say a few words of him we now commemorate. Mr. Justice Story, in an address delivered on the occasion of his death, speaks "of those exquisite judgments, the fruits of his own unassisted meditations, from which the court has received so much honor," and I have sometimes thought even the bar of the country hardly realizes to what extent he was, in some respects, unassisted. He was appointed Chief Justice in January, 1801, and took his seat on the bench at the following February term. The court had then been in existence but eleven years, and in that time less than one hundred cases had passed under its judgment. The engrossed minutes of its doings cover only a little more than two hundred pages of one of the volumes of its records, and its reported decisions fill but five hundred pages of three volumes of the reports published by Mr. Dallas. The courts of the several colonies before the Revolution, and of the States afterwards, had done all that was required of them, and yet the volumes of their decisions published before 1801 can be counted on little more than the fingers of a single hand, and if these and all the cases decided before that time, which have been reported since, were put into volumes of the size now issued by the reporter of the Supreme Court, it would not require the fingers of both the hands for their full enumeration. The reported decisions of all the circuit and district courts of the United States were put into a little more than two hundred pages of Dallas.

In this condition of the jurisprudence of the country MARSHALL took his place at the head of the national judiciary. The Government, under the Constitution, was only organized twelve years before, and in the interval eleven amendments of the Constitution had been regularly proposed and adopted. Comparatively nothing had been done judicially to define the powers or develop the resources of the Constitution. The common law of the mother country had been either silently or by express enactment adopted as the foundation of the system by which the rights of persons and property were to be determined, but scarcely anything had been done by the courts to adapt it to the new form of government, or to the new relations of social life which a successful revolution had produced. In short, the nation, the Constitution, and the laws were in their infancy. Under these circumstances it was most fortunate for the country that the great Chief Justice retained his high position for thirty-four years, and that during all that time, with scarcely any interruption, he kept on with the work he showed himself so competent to perform. As year after year went by and new occasion required, with his irresistible logic, enforced by his cogent English, he developed the hidden treasures of the Constitution, demonstrated its capacities, and showed beyond all possibility of doubt that a government rightfully administered under

2 M

its authority could protect itself against itself and against the world. He kept himself at the front on all questions of constitutional law, and, consequently, his master hand is seen in every case which involved that subject. At the same time he and his co-workers, whose names are, some of them, almost as familiar as his own, were engaged in laying, deep and strong, the foundations on which the jurisprudence of the country has since been built. Hardly a day now passes in the court he so dignified and adorned without reference to some decision of his time as establishing a principle which, from that day to this, has been accepted as undoubted law.

It is not strange that this is so. Great as he was, he was made greater by those about him, and the events in the midst of which he lived. He sat with Paterson, with Bushrod Washington, with William

Johnson, with Livingston, with Story, and with Thompson, and there came before him Webster and Pinkney and Wirt and Dexter and Sergeant and Binney and Martin, and many others equally illustrious, who then made up the bar of the Supreme Court. He was a giant among giants. Abundance of time was taken for consideration. Judgments, when announced, were the result of deliberate thought and patient investigation, and opinions were never filed until they had been prepared with the greatest care. The first volume of Cranch's Reports embraces the work of two full years, and all the opinions save one are from the pen of the Chief Justice. Twenty-five cases only are reported, but among them is Marbury *v.* Madison, in which, for the first time, it was announced by the Supreme Court that it was the duty of the judiciary to declare an act of the legislative

department of the Government invalid if
clearly repugnant to the Constitution.

After this came, in quick succession, all
the various questions of constitutional, in-
ternational, and general law which would
naturally present themselves for judicial
determination in a new and rapidly developing country. The complications grow-
ing out of the wars in Europe, and of
our own war with Great Britain, brought
up their disputes for settlement, and the
boundary line between the powers of the
States and of the United States had more
than once to be run and marked. The
authority of the United States was extended by treaty over territory not origi-
nally within its jurisdiction. All these
involved the consideration of subjects
comparatively new in the domain of the
law, and rights were to be settled, not on
authorities alone, but by the application of
the principles of right reason. Here the

Chief Justice was at home, and when, at the end of his long and eminent career he laid down his life, he, and those who had so ably assisted him in his great work, had the right to say that the judicial power of the United States had been carefully preserved and wisely administered. The nation can never honor him, or them, too much for the work they accomplished.

Without detaining you longer, I ask you to look upon what is hereafter to represent, at the seat of government, the reverence of the Congress and the bar of the United States for JOHN MARSHALL, "The Expounder of the Constitution."

William Henry Rawle, Esq., of Philadelphia, then delivered the following oration:

JOHN MARSHALL, Chief Justice of the United States, has been dead for nearly half a century, and if it be asked why at this late day we have come together to do tardy justice to his memory and unveil this statue in his honor, the answer may be given in a few words. The history dates from his death. He had held his last Court, and had come northward to seek medical aid in the city of Philadelphia, and there, on the 6th of July, 1835, he died. While tributes of respect for the man and of grief for the national loss were paid throughout the country, it was felt by the Bar of the city where he died that a lasting monument should be erected to his memory in the capital of the nation. To this end subscriptions, limited in amount, were asked. About half came from the Bar of Philadelphia, and of the rest, the largest

contribution was from the city of Richmond, but all told, the sum was utterly
insufficient. What money there was, was
invested by trustees as "THE MARSHALL
MEMORIAL FUND," and then the matter
seemed to pass out of men's minds.
Nearly fifty years went on. Another generation and still another came into the
world, till lately, on the death of the survivor of the trustees, himself an old man,
the late Peter McCall, the almost forgotten
fund was found to have been increased, by
honest stewardship, seven-fold. Of the
original subscribers but six were known
to be alive, and upon their application
trustees were appointed to apply the fund
to its original purpose. It happened that
at this time the Forty-seventh Congress
appropriated of the people's money a sum
about equal in amount for the erection of
a statue to the memory of Chief Justice
MARSHALL, to be "placed in a suitable

public reservation in the city of Washington." To serve their common purpose, the Congressional committee and the trustees agreed to unite in the erection of a statue and pedestal; and after much thought and care the commission was intrusted to William W. Story, an artist who brought to the task not only his acknowledged genius, but a keen desire to perpetuate through the work of his hands the face and form of one who had been not only his father's professional brother but the object of his chiefest respect and admiration. That work now stands before you. Its pedestal bears the simple inscription:—

JOHN MARSHALL

CHIEF JUSTICE OF THE UNITED STATES

ERECTED BY

THE BAR AND THE CONGRESS

OF THE UNITED STATES

A. D. MDCCCLXXXIV.

No more "suitable public reservation" could be found than the ground on which we stand, almost within the shadow of the Capitol in which for more than thirty years he held the highest judicial position in the country.

It may well be that the even tenor of his judicial life has driven from some minds the story of his brilliant and eventful youth.   The same simplicity, the same modesty which marked the child distinguished the great Chief Justice, but, as a judge, his life was necessarily one of thought and study, of enforced retirement from much of the busy world, dealing more with results than processes; and the surges of faction and of passion, the heat of ambition, the thirst of power, reached him not in his high judicial station.   Yet he had himself been a busy actor on the scenes of life, and if his later days seemed colorless, the story of his earlier years is full of charm.

The eldest of a large family, reared in Fauquier County, in Virginia, he was one of the tenderest, the most lovable of children. He had never, said his father, seriously displeased him in his life. To his mother, to his sisters especially, did he bear that chivalrous devotion which to the last hour of his life he showed to women. Such education as came to him was little got from schools, for the thinly-settled country and his father's limited means forbade this. A year's Latin at fourteen at a school a hundred miles from his home, and another year's Latin at home with the rector of the parish was the sum of his classical teaching. What else of it he learned was with the unsympathetic aid of grammar and dictionary. But his father— who, MARSHALL was wont to say, was a far abler man than any of his sons, and who in early life was Washington's companion as a land surveyor, and, later, fought gallantly under him—his father was well read in English literature, and loved to open its treasures to the quick, receptive mind of his eldest child, who in it all, especially in history and still more in poetry, found an enduring delight. Much of his time was passed in the open air, among the hills and valleys of that beautiful country, and thus it was that in active exercise, in day dreams of heroism and poetry, in rapid and eager mastery of such learning as came within his reach, and surrounded by the tender love, the idolatry of a happy family, his earlier days were passed.

The first note of war that rang through the land called him to arms, and from 1775, when was his first battle on the soil of his own State, until the end of 1779, he was in the army. Through the battles of Iron Hill, of Brandywine, of Germantown and of Monmouth, he bore himself bravely, and

through the dreary privations, the hunger
and the nakedness of that ghastly winter at
Valley Forge, his patient endurance and
his cheeriness bespoke the very sweetest
temper that ever man was blessed with.
So long as any lived to speak, men would
tell how he was loved by the soldiers and
by his brother officers; how he was the
arbiter of their differences and the com-
poser of their disputes, and when called
to act, as he often was, as judge advocate,
he exercised that peculiar and delicate
judgment required of him who is not only
the prosecutor but the protector of the
accused. It was in the duties of this office
that he first met and came to know well
the two men whom of all others on earth
he most admired and loved, and whose
impress he bore through his life, Washington and Hamilton.

While of MARSHALL's life war was but
.the brief opening episode, yet before we

leave these days, one part of them has a peculiar charm. There were more officers than were needed, and he had come back to his home. His letters from camp had been read with delight by his sisters and his sisters' friends. His reputation as a soldier had preceded him, and the daughters of Virginia, then, as ever, ready to welcome those who do service to the State, greeted him with their sweetest smiles. One of these was a shy, diffident girl of fourteen; and to the amazement of all, and perhaps to her own, from that time his devotion to her knew no variableness neither shadow of turning. She afterwards became his wife, and for fifty years, in sickness and in health, he loved and cherished her till, as he himself said, "her sainted spirit fled from the sufferings of life." When her release came at last, he mourned her as he had loved her, and the years were few before he followed her to the grave.

But from this happy home he tore himself away, and at the College of William and Mary attended a course of law lectures and in due time was admitted to practice. But practice there was none, for Arnold had then invaded Virginia, and it was literally true that *inter arma silent leges.* To resist the invasion, MARSHALL returned to the army, and at its end, there being still a redundance of officers in the Virginia line, he resigned his commission and again took up his studies. With the return of peace the courts were opened and his career at the bar began. Tradition tells how even at that early day his characteristic traits began to show themselves—his simple, quiet bearing, his frankness and candor, his marvellous grasp of principle, his power of clear statement and his logical reasoning. It is pleasant to know that his rapid rise excited no envy among his associates, for his other high qualities were exceeded by his modesty. In after life this modesty was wont to attribute his success to the "too partial regard of his former companions-in-arms, who, at the end of the war, had returned to their families and were scattered over the States." But the cause was in himself, and not in his friends.

In the spring of 1782 he was elected to the State legislature, and in the autumn chosen to the Executive Council. In the next year took place his happy marriage, his removal to Richmond, thenceforth his home, and soon after, his retirement, as he supposed, from public life. But this was not to be, for his election again and again to the legislature called on him for service which he was too patriotic to withhold, even had he felt less keenly how full of trouble were the times. MARSHALL threw himself, heart and soul, into the great questions which bade fair to destroy by dissension

what had been won by arms, and opposed
to the best talent of his own State, he
ranged himself with an unpopular minor-
ity. In measured words, years later, when
he wrote the life of Washington, he defined
the issue which then threatened to tear the
country asunder. It was, he said, "divided into two great political parties, the
one of which contemplated America as a
nation, and labored incessantly to invest
the Federal head with powers competent
to the preservation of the Union. The
other attached itself to the State government, viewed all the powers of Congress
with jealousy, and assented reluctantly to
measures which would enable the head to
act in any respect independently of the
members." Though the proposed Constitution might form, as its preamble declares,
"a more perfect union" than had the Ar-
ticles of Confederation; though it might
prevent anarchy and save the States from

becoming secret or open enemies of each
other; though it might replace "a Government depending upon thirteen distinct
sovereignties for the preservation of the
public faith" by one whose power might
regulate and control them all—the more
numerous and powerful, and certainly the
more clamorous party insisted that such
evils, and evils worse than these, were
as nothing compared to the surrender of
State independence to Federal sovereignty.
In public and private, in popular meet-
ings, in legislatures and in conventions,
on both sides passion was mingled with
argument. Notably in MARSHALL'S own
State did many of her ablest sons, then and
afterwards most dear to her, throw all that
they had of courage, of high character and
of patriotism, into the attempt to save the
young country from its threatened yoke
of despotism. Equally brave and able
were those few who led the other party,

and chief among them were Washington,
Madison, Randolph and, later, MARSHALL.
Young as he was, it was felt that such a
man could not be left out of the State convention to which the Constitution was to
be submitted, but he was warned by his
best friends that unless he should pledge
himself to oppose it his defeat was certain.
He said plainly that, if elected, he should
be "a determined advocate for its adoption,"
and his integrity and fearlessness overcame
even the prejudices of his constituents.
And in that memorable debate, which
lasted five-and-twenty days, though with
his usual modesty he contented himself
with supporting the lead of Madison, three
times he came to the front, and to the
questions of the power of taxation, the
power over the militia and the power of
the judiciary, he brought the full force of
his fast developing strength. The contest
was severe and the vote close. The Con-

stitution was ratified by a majority of only
ten. But as to MARSHALL, it has been truly
said that "in sustaining the Constitution,
he unconsciously prepared for his own
glory the imperishable connection which
his name now has with its principles."
And again his modesty would have it that
he builded better than he knew, for in later
times he would ascribe the course which he
took to casual circumstances as much as
to judgment; he had early, he said, caught
up the words, "United we stand, divided
we fall"; the feelings they inspired became
a part of his being; he carried them into
the army where, associating with brave
men from different States who were risk-
ing life and all else in a common cause, he
was confirmed in the habit of considering
America as his country, and Congress as
his Government.

The convention was held in 1788. Again
MARSHALL was sent to the legislature,

where in power of logical debate he confessedly led the House, until in 1792 he left it finally.

During the next five years he was at the height of his professional reputation. The Federal reports and those of his own State show that among a Bar distinguished almost beyond all others, he was engaged in most of the important cases of the time. A few of these he has reported himself; they are modestly inserted at the end of the volume, and are referred to by the reporter as contributed "by a gentleman high in practice at the time, and by whose permission they are now published."

And here a word must be said as to the nature and extent of his technical learning, for it is almost without parallel that one should admittedly have held the highest position at the Bar, and then for thirty-five years should, as admittedly, have held the reputation of a great judge, when the en-

tire time between the very commencement
of his studies and his relinquishment of
practice was less than seventeen years. In
that generation of lawyers and the generation which succeeded them, it was not un-
usual that more than half that time passed
before they had either a cause or a client.
MARSHALL had emphatically what is called
a legal mind; his marvellous instinct as to
what the law *ought* to be doubtless saved
him much labor which was necessary to
those less intellectually great. With the
principles of the science he was of course
familiar; with their sources he was scarcely
less so. A century ago there was less law
to be learned and men learned it more completely. Except as to such addition as has
of late years come to us from the civil law,
the foundation of it was the same as now
—the same common law, the same decisions, the same statutes—and in that day, a
century's separation from the mother coun-

try had wrought little change in the colonies except to adapt this law to their local needs with marvellous skill. Save as to this, the law of the one country was the law of the other, and the decisions at Westminster Hall before the Revolution were of as much authority here as there. There was not a single published volume of American reports. The enormous superstructure which has since been raised upon the same foundation, bewildering from its height, the number of its stories, the vast number of its chambers, the intricacies of its passages, has been a necessity from the growth of a country rapid beyond precedent in a century to which history knows no parallel. But the foundation of it was the same, and the men of the last century had not far to go beyond the foundation, and hence their technical learning was, as to some at least, more complete, if not more profound. There were a few who said that MARSHALL was never what is called a thoroughly technical lawyer. If by this is meant that he never mistook the grooves and ruts of the law for the law itself—that he looked at the law from above and not from below, and did not cite precedent where citation was not necessary— the remark might have semblance of truth, but the same might be said of his noted abstinence from illustration and analogy, both of which he could, upon occasion, call in aid; but no one can read those arguments at the Bar or judgments on the bench in which he thought it needful to establish his propositions by technical precedents, without feeling that he possessed as well the knowledge of their existence and the reason of their existence, as the power to analyze them. But he never mistook the means for the end.

Even in the height of his prosperous labor he never turned his back upon public duty. Not all the excesses of the French revolution could make the mass of Americans forget that France had been our ally in the war with England, and when, in 1793, these nations took arms against each other, and our proclamation of neutrality was issued to the world, loud and deep were the curses that rang through the land. Hated as the proclamation was, MARSHALL had no doubt of its wisdom. Great was his grief to oppose himself to the judgment of Madison, but he was content to share the odium heaped upon Hamilton and Washington, and to be denounced as an aristocrat, a loyalist and an enemy to republicanism. With rare courage, at a public meeting at Richmond he defended the wisdom and policy of the administration, and his argument as to the Constitutionality of the proclamation anticipated the judgment of the world.

Two years later came a severer trial.

Without his knowledge and against his
will, MARSHALL had been again elected to
the legislature. Our minister to Great
Britain had concluded a commercial treaty
with that power, and its ratification had
been advised by the Senate and acted on
by the President. The indignation of the
people knew no bounds. In no State was
it greater than in Virginia. The treaty was
"insulting to the dignity, injurious to the
interests, dangerous to the security and repugnant to the Constitution of the United
States"—so said the resolutions of a remarkable meeting at Richmond, and these
words echoed through the country. Had
not the Constitution given to Congress the
right to regulate commerce, and how dared
the Executive, without Congress, negotiate
a treaty of commerce? MARSHALL'S friends
begged him, for his own sake, not to stem
the popular torrent. He hoped at first that
his own legislature might, as he wrote to

Hamilton from Richmond, "ultimately consult the interest or honor of the nation. But now," he went on to say, "when all hope of this had vanished, it was deemed advisable to make the experiment, however hazardous it might be. A meeting was called which was more numerous than I have ever seen at this place; and after a very ardent and zealous discussion, which consumed the day, a decided majority declared in favor of a resolution that the welfare and honor of the nation required us to give full effect to the treaty negotiated with Britain." Thus measuredly he told the story of one of his greatest triumphs, and afterwards, in his place in the House, he again met the Constitutional objection in a speech which, men said at the time, was even stronger than the other. As he spoke, reason asserted her sway over passion, party feeling gave way to conviction, and for once the vote of the House was

turned. Of this speech no recorded trace
remains, but even in that time, when news
travelled slowly, its fame spread abroad,
and the subsequent conduct of every administration has to this day rested upon
the construction then given to the Constitution by MARSHALL.

Henceforth his reputation became national, and when, a few months later, he
came to Philadelphia to argue the great
case of the confiscation by Virginia of the
British debts, a contemporary said of him,
"Speaking, as he always does, to the judgment merely, and for the simple purpose
of convincing, he was justly pronounced
one of the greatest men in the country."
He were less than human not to be moved
by this, but, in writing to a friend, he modestly said, "A Virginian who supported
with any sort of reputation the measures
of the Government was such a *rara avis*
that I was received with a degree of kind-

ness which I had not anticipated." Soon
after, Washington offered him the position
of Attorney-General, and some months
later, the mission to France. Both he declined. His determination to remain at
the Bar, was, he thought, unalterable.

And again he altered it. Our relations
with France had drifted from friendship to
coolness, and from coolness to almost war.
Neither France herself nor the "French
patriots" here had forgotten or forgiven
the treaty with Great Britain, and if the
disgust at our persistent neutrality did not
break into open war, it was because France
knew, or thought she knew, that the entire
American opposition to the Government
was on her side. Just short of war she
stopped. Privateers fitted out by orders
of the French minister here preyed upon
our commerce; the very ship which brought
him to our shores began to capture our
vessels before even his credentials had

been presented; later, by order of the
Directory, he suspended his diplomatic
funćtions here and flung to our people
turgid words of bitterness as he left; the
minister whom we had sent to France
when MARSHALL had declined to go, was
not only not received, but was ordered out
of the country and threatened with the
police. The crisis required the greatest
wisdom and firmness which the country
could command. Mr. Adams was then
President; he never lacked firmness, and
his words to Congress at its special session
were full of fearless dignity. "Three envoys," said he, "persons of talents and
integrity, long known and intrusted in the
three great divisions of the Union," were
to be sent to France, and MARSHALL was
to be one of them. It went hard with him,
but the struggle was short, and as he left
his home at Richmond crowds of citizens
attended him for miles, and all party feel-

ing was merged in respect and affection. The issue of his errand belongs to history. He has himself told us, in his Life of Washington, how the envoys—his own name being characteristically withheld— were met by contumely and insult; how the wiliest minister of the age suggested that a large sum of money must be paid to the Directory as a mere preliminary to negotiation; how, if they refused, it would be known at home that they were corrupted by British influence, and how insults and menaces were borne with equal dignity. But he has not told us that his were the two letters to Talleyrand which have justly been regarded as among the ablest State papers in diplomacy. They were unanswerable, and nothing remained but to get MARSHALL and one of his colleagues out of the country with as little delay as was consistent with additional marks of contempt. His return showed that republics are not always ungrateful, for there came out to him on his arrival a crowd even greater than that which had witnessed his departure, the Secretary of State and other officials among them, and at a celebration in his honor the phrase was coined which afterwards became national, "Millions for defense, but not one cent for tribute."

Now, surely, he had earned the right to return to his loved professional labor. Nor only this—he had earned the right to such honor as the dignified labor of high judicial station could alone afford. The position of Justice of the Supreme Court of the United States had fallen vacant, and the President's choice rested on MAR-SHALL. "He has raised the American people in their own esteem," wrote Mr. Adams to the Secretary of State, "and if the influence of truth and justice, reason and argument, is not lost in Europe, he has raised the consideration of the United

States in that quarter." But again there had come to him the call of duty. For Washington, who, in view of the expected war with France, had been appointed to command the army, had begged MAR-SHALL to come to him at Mount Vernon, and there in earnest talk for days dwelt upon the importance to the country that he should be returned to Congress. His reluctance was great not only to re-enter public life, but to throw himself into a con-test sure to be marked with an intensity of public excitement, degenerating into pri-vate calumny. If Washington himself had not escaped this, how should he?

The canvass began. In the midst of it came the offer of the repose and dignity of the Supreme Bench. But his word had been given and he at once declined. The contest was severe, his majority was small, and his election, though intensely grateful to Washington and those who ·thought

4 M

with him, was met with many misgivings
from some who thought him "too much
disposed to govern the world according to
rules of logic."

His first act in Congress was to an-
nounce the death of Washington, and the
words of the resolutions which he then
presented, though written by another,
meet our eyes on every hand, "First in
war, first in peace, and first in the hearts
of his countrymen." It was like MAR-
SHALL that when later he came to write
the life of Washington, he should have
said that the resolutions were presented
by "a member of the House."

In that House—the last Congress that
sat in Philadelphia—he met the ablest men
of the country. New member as he was,
when the debate involved questions of law
or the Constitution he was confessedly the
first man in it. His speech on the question of Nash's surrender is said to be the

only one ever revised by him, and, as it
stands, is a model of parliamentary argument. The President had advised the
surrender of the prisoner to the English
Government to answer a charge of murder
on the high seas on board a British man-
of-war. Popular outcry insisted that the
prisoner was an American, unlawfully impressed, and that the death was caused in
his attempt to regain his freedom; and
though this was untrue, it was urged that
as the case involved principles of law, the
question of surrender was one for judicial
and not Executive decision. In most of its
aspects the subject was confessedly new,
but it was exhausted by MARSHALL. Not
every case, he showed, which involves
principles of law necessarily came before
the courts; the parties here were two
nations, who could not litigate their
claims; the demand was not a case for
judicial cognizance; the treaty under which

the surrender was made was a law en-
joining the performance of a particular
object; the department to perform it was
the Executive, who, under the Constitution, was to "take care that the laws be
faithfully executed"; and even if Congress
had not yet prescribed the particular mode
by which this was to be done, it was not
the less the duty of the Executive to execute it by any means it then possessed.

There was no answer to this, worthy the
name; the member selected to answer it
sat silent; the resolutions against the erection were lost, and thus the power was
lodged where it should belong, and an
unwelcome and inappropriate jurisdiction
diverted from the judiciary.

The session was just over when, in May,
the President, without consulting MAR-
SHALL, appointed him Secretary of War.
He wrote to decline. As part of the well-
known disruption of the Cabinet the office

of Secretary of State became vacant, and MARSHALL was appointed to and accepted it. During his short tenure of office, an occasion arose for the display of his best powers, in his dispatch to our minister to England concerning questions of great moment under our treaty, of contraband, blockade, impressment, and compensation to British subjects, a State paper not surpassed by any in the archives of that Department.

The autumn of 1800 witnessed the defeat of Mr. Adams for the Presidency and the resignation of Chief Justice Ellsworth, and, at MARSHALL'S suggestion, Chief Justice Jay was invited to return to his former position, but declined. On being again consulted, MARSHALL urged the appointment of Mr. Justice Paterson, then on the Supreme Bench. Some said that the vacant office might possibly be filled by the President himself after the 3d of

March, but Mr. Adams disclaimed the idea.
"I have already," wrote he, "by the nomi-
nation to this office of a gentleman in full
vigor of middle life, in the full habits of
business, and whose reading in the science
of law is fresh in his head, put it wholly
out of my power, and indeed it never was
in my hópes and wishes;" and on the 31st
of January, 1801, the President requested
the Secretary of War "to execute the office
of Secretary of State so far as to affix the
seal of the United States to the inclosed
commission to the present Secretary of
State, JOHN MARSHALL of Virginia, to be
Chief Justice of the United States." He
was then forty-six years old.

It is difficult for the present generation
to appreciate the contrast between the Supreme Court to which MARSHALL came
and the Supreme Court as he left it; the
contrast is scarcely less between the Court
as he left it and the Court of to-day. For

the first time in the history of the world
had a written constitution become an or-
ganic law of government; for the first time
was such an instrument to be submitted
to judgment. With admirable force Mr.
Gladstone has said, "As the British Constitution is the most subtile organism
which has proceeded from progressive
history, so the American Constitution is
the most wonderful work ever struck off
at a given time by the brain and purpose
of man." On that subtile and unwritten
Constitution of England, the professional
training of every older lawyer in the
country had been based, and they had
learned from it that the power of Parlia-
ment was above and beyond the judgments of any court in the realm. Though
this American Constitution declared in so
many words that the judicial power should
extend to "all cases arising under the
Constitution and the laws of the United

States," yet it was difficult for men so
trained to conceive how any law which the
Legislative department might pass and the
Executive approve could be set aside by the
mere judgment of a court. There was no
precedent for it in ancient or modern history. Hence when first this question was
suggested in a Federal court, it was received with grave misgiving; the general
principles of the Constitution were not, it
was said, to be regarded as rules to fetter
and control, but as matter merely declara-
tory and directory; and even if legislative
acts directly contrary to it *should* be void,
whose was the power to declare them so?

Equally without precedent was every
other question. Those who, in their places
as legislators, had fought the battle of
State sovereignty, were ready to urge in
the courts of justice that the Federal Government could claim no powers that had
not been delegated to it *in ipsissimis*

verbis. If delegated at all, they were to be contracted by construction within the narrowest limits. Whether the right of Congress to pass all laws "necessary and proper" for the Federal Government was not restricted to such as were indispensable to that end; whether the right of taxation could be exercised by a State against creations of the Federal Government; whether a Federal court could revise the judgment of a State court in a case arising under the Constitution and laws of the United States; whether the officers of the Federal Government could be protected against State interference; how far extended the power of Congress to regulate commerce within the States; how far to regulate foreign commerce as against State enactment; how far extended the prohibition to the States against emitting bills of credit—these and like questions were absolutely without precedent.

It is not too much to say that but for MARSHALL such questions could hardly have been solved as they were. There have been great judges before and since, but none had ever such opportunity, and none ever seized and improved it as he did. For, as was said by our late President, "He found the Constitution paper, and he made it power; he found it a skeleton, and clothed it with flesh and blood." Not in a few feeble words at such a time as this can be told how, with easy power he grasped the momentous questions as they arose; how his great statesmanship lifted them to a high plane; how his own clear vision pierced clouds which caused others to see as through a glass darkly, and how all that his wisdom could conceive and his reason could prove was backed by a judicial courage unequalled in history.

It may be doubted whether, great as is

his reputation, full justice has yet been done him. In his interpretation of the law, the premises seem so undeniable, the reasoning so logical, the conclusions so irresistible, that men are wont to wonder that there had ever been any question at all.

A single instance—the first which arose —may tell its own story. Congress had given to his own court a jurisdiction not within the range of its powers under the Constitution. If it could lawfully do this, the case before the court was plain. Whether it could, said the court, in MARSHALL'S words, "Whether an act repugnant to the Constitution can become the law of the land, is a question deeply interesting to the United States, but, happily, not of an intricacy proportioned to its interest;" and in these few words was the demonstration made: "It is a proposition too plain to be contested, that the

Constitution controls any legislative act repugnant to it, or that the legislature can alter the Constitution by an ordinary act. Between these alternatives there is no middle ground. The Constitution is either a superior paramount law, unchangeable by ordinary means, or it is on a level with ordinary legislative acts, and, like other acts, is alterable when the legislature shall please to alter it. If the former part of the alternative be true, then a legislative act contrary to the Constitution is not law; if the latter part be true, then written constitutions are absurd attempts on the part of the people to limit a power in its own nature illimitable."

Here was established one of the great foundation principles of the Government, and then in a few sentences, and for the first time, was clearly and tersely stated the theory of the Constitution as to the separate powers of the Legislature and the

Judiciary. If, he said, its theory was that
an act of the Legislature repugnant to it
was void, such an act could not bind the
courts and oblige them to give it effect.
This would be to overthrow in fact what
was established in theory. It was of the
very essence of judicial duty to expound
and interpret the law; to determine which
of two conflicting laws should prevail.
When a law came in conflict with the
Constitution, the judicial department must
decide between them. Otherwise, the
courts must close their eyes on the Constitution, which they were sworn to sup-
port, and see only the law

The exposition thus begun was continued for more than thirty years, and in
a series of judgments, contained in many
volumes, is to be found the basis of what
is to-day the constitutional law of this
country. Were it possible, it would be
inappropriate to follow here, with what-

ever profit, the processes by which this great work was done. The least approach to technical analysis would demand a statement of the successive questions as they arose, each fraught with the history of the time and each suggesting illustrations and analogies which subsequent time has developed. It may have been that could MARSHALL have foreseen the extent to which, in some instances, his conclusions could be carried, in the uncertain future and under such wholly changed circumstances as no man could then conjecture, he would possibly have qualified or limited their application; but the marvel is, that of all he wrought in the field of constitutional labor there is so little that admits of even question.

But besides this, there was much more. It has been truly said of him that he would have been a great judge at any time and in any country. Great in the

sense in which Nottingham and Hard-
wicke as to equity were great; in which
Mansfield as to commercial law and Stow-
ell as to admiralty were great—great in
that, with little precedent to guide them,
they produced a system with which the
wisdom of succeeding generations has
found little fault and has little changed.
In MARSHALL'S court there was little precedent by which to determine the rights
of the Indian tribes over the land which
had once been theirs, or their rights as
nations against the States in which they
dwelt; there was little precedent when,
beyond the seas, the heat of war had produced the British Orders in Council and
the retaliatory Berlin and Milan Decrees;
when the conflicting rights of neutrals and
belligerents, of captors and claimants, of
those trading under the flag of peace and
those privateering under letters of marque
and reprisal; when the effect of the judg-

ments of foreign tribunals; when the
jurisdiction of the sovereign upon the
high seas—when these and similar questions arose, there was little precedent for
their solution, and they had to be considered upon broad and general principles
of jurisprudence, and the result has been
a code for future time.

Passing from this, a word must be said
as to his judicial conduct when sitting
apart from his brethren in his Circuit
Courts. Especially when presiding over
trials by jury his best personal character-
istics were shown. The dignity, maintained
without effort, which forbade the possibility of unseemly difference, the quick
comprehension, the unfailing patience, the
prompt ruling, the serene impartiality, and,
when required, the most absolute courage
and independence, made up as nearly perfect a judge at Nisi Prius as the world has
ever known.

One instance only can be noticed here.
The story of Aaron Burr, with all its
reality and all its romance, must always,
spite of much that is repugnant, fascinate
both young and old. When, in a phase of
his varied life, he who had been noted, if
not famous, as a soldier, as a lawyer, as an
orator, who had won the reason of men
and charmed the hearts of women, who
had held the high office of Vice-President
of the United States, and whose hands
were red with the blood of Hamilton—
when he found himself on trial for his life
upon the charge of high treason, before a
judge who was Hamilton's dear friend and
a jury chosen with difficulty from an excited people, what wonder that, like Cain,
he felt himself singled out from his fellows,
and, coming between his counsel and the
court, exclaimed: "Would to God that I
did stand on the same ground with any
other man!" And yet the impartiality

5 M

which marked the conduct of those trials
was never excelled in history. By the
law of our mother country to have only
compassed and imagined the government's subversion was treason; but, according to our Constitution, "treason
against the United States shall consist
only in levying war against them, or in
adhering to their enemies, giving them
aid and comfort," and can it be, said MAR-
SHALL, that the landing of a few men,
however desperate and however intent to
overthrow the government of a State, was
a levying of war? It might be a conspir-
acy, but it was not treason within the Constitution—and Burr's accomplices were dis-
charged of their high crime. And upon his
own memorable trial—that strange scene
in which these men, the prisoner and the
judge, each so striking in appearance, were
confronted, and as people said, "two such
pairs of eyes had never looked into one

another before"—upon that trial the scales of justice were held with absolutely even hand. No greater display of judicial skill and judicial rectitude was ever witnessed. No more effective dignity ever added weight to judicial language. Outside the court and through the country it was cried that "the people of America demanded a conviction," and within it all the pressure which counsel dared to borrow was exerted to this end. It could hardly be passed by. "That this court dares not usurp power, is most true," began the last lines of MARSHALL'S charge to the jury. "That this court dares not shrink from its duty, is not less true. No man is desirous of becoming the peculiar subject of calumny. No man, might he let the bitter cup pass from him without self-reproach, would drain it to the bottom. But if he have no choice in the case, if there be no alternative presented to him but a dereliction of duty or the opprobrium of those who are denominated the world, he merits the contempt as well as the indignation of his country, who can hesitate which to embrace." That counsel should, he said, be impatient at any deliberation of the court, and suspect or fear the operation of motives to which alone they could ascribe that deliberation, was perhaps a frailty incident to human nature, "but if any conduct could warrant a sentiment that it would deviate to the one side or the other from the line prescribed by duty and by law, that conduct would be viewed by the judges themselves with an eye of extreme severity, and would long be recollected with deep and serious regrets."

The result was acquittal, and as was said by the angry counsel for the Government, " MARSHALL has stepped in between Burr and death!" Though the disappointment was extreme; though starting

from the level of excited popular feeling, it
made its way upward till it reached the dignity of grave dissatisfaction expressed in
a President's message to Congress; though
the trial led to legislative alteration of the
law, the judge was unmoved by criticism,
no matter from what quarter, and was content to await the judgment of posterity
that never, in all the dark history of
State trials, was the law, as then it stood
and bound both parties, ever interpreted
with more impartiality to the accuser and
the accused.

Once only did MARSHALL enter the
field of authorship. Washington had be-
queathed all his papers, public and pri-
vate, to his favorite nephew, who was one
of MARSHALL's associates on the bench.
It was agreed between them that Judge
Washington should contribute the material
and that MARSHALL should prepare the
biography. The bulk of papers was enor-

mous, and MARSHALL had just taken his
seat on the bench and was deep in judicial work. The task was done under severe pressure, and ill health more than
once interrupted it; but it was a labor of
love, and his whole heart went out toward
the subject. His political opponents feared
that his strong convictions, which he never
concealed, would now be turned to the
account of his party, but the writer was
as impartial as the judge. He recalled
and perpetuated the intrigues and cabals,
the disappointments and the griefs which,
equally with the successes, were part of
Washington's life; but full justice was
done to those men whom both Washington and his biographer distrusted and opposed. It is agreed that for minuteness,
impartiality, and accuracy, the history is
exceeded by none. There were those who
said the work was colorless, and others
were severe by reason of the absolute

truth which became their most absolute punishment, but no one's judgment was as severe as MARSHALL'S own, save only as to its accuracy. Once only was this seriously questioned, and by one of the most distinguished of his opponents, and the result was complete vindication.

It is matter of history that upon Washington's death the House had resolved that a marble monument should be erected in the city of Washington, "so designed as to commemorate the great events of his military and political life." But, as MAR-SHALL tells us, "that those great events should be commemorated could not be pleasing to those who had condemned, and continued to condemn, the whole course of his administration." The resolution was postponed in the Senate and never passed, and almost the only tinge of bitterness in his pages is that those who possessed the ascendency over the public sentiment employed their influence "to impress the idea that the only proper monument to a meritorious citizen was that which the people would erect in their affections." This he wrote in 1807 and repeated in 1832, and in the next year the people resolved that this should no longer be. The National Monument Association was then formed, and MARSHALL was its first president. Under its auspices, and with the aid, long after, of large appropriations by Congress, the gigantic column within our sight is slowly and gradually being reared.

Near the close of his life, when he was seventy-four years old, MARSHALL was chosen a member of the convention which met, in 1829, to revise the constitution of his native State. It was a remarkable body. The best men of the State were there. Some of them were among the best men in the country, for then, as always, Virginia had been proud to rear and send forth men whose names were foremost in their country's history. Prominent among them were Madison, Monroe and MARSHALL. Even then, party spirit ran high. Two questions in particular, the basis of representation and the tenure of judicial office, distracted the convention as they had distracted the people. On both these questions MARSHALL spoke with his accustomed dignity and not less than his accustomed force, and his words were listened to with reverent respect. Upon the subject of judicial tenure he spoke from his very heart, "with the fervor and almost the authority of an apostle." He knew, better than any, how a judge, standing between the powerful and the powerless, was bound to deal justice to both, and that to this end his own position should be beyond the reach of anything mortal. "The judicial department," said he, "comes home in its effects to every man's fireside; it passes on his property, his reputation, his life, his all. Is it not to the last degree important that he should be rendered perfectly and completely independent, with nothing to control him but God and his conscience?" And his next words were fraught with the wisdom of past ages, let us hope not with prophetic foreboding: "I have always thought, from my earliest youth till now, that the greatest scourge an angry Heaven ever inflicted upon an ungrateful and a sinning people, was an ignorant, a corrupt, or a dependent judiciary."

Something has here been said of Marshall's inner life in its earlier years, and no man's life was ever more dear to those around him than was his from its beginning to its close. His singleness and simplicity of character, his simplicity of living, his love for the young and respect

for the old, his deference to women, his
courteous bearing, his tender charity, his
reluctance to conceive offense and his read-
iness to forgive it, have become traditions
from which in our memories of him we in-
terweave all that we most look up to, with
all that we take most nearly to our hearts.

As the evening of life cast its long
shadows before him, the labor and sorrow
that come with four-score years were not
allowed to pass him by. Great physical
suffering came to him; the hours not
absorbed in work brought to him memories of her whose life had been one with
his for fifty years. The "great simple
heart, too brave to be ashamed of tears,"
was too brave not to confess that rarely
did he go through a night without shed-
ding them for her. No outward trace of
this betrayed itself, but lest some part of
it should, all unconsciously to himself,
impair his mental force, he begged those

nearest to him to tell him in plain words
when any signs of failing should appear.
But the steady light within burned brightly
to the last, however waning might be his
mortal strength. He met his end, not at
his home, but surrounded by those most
dear to him. As it drew near, he wrote
the simple inscription to be placed upon
his grave. His parentage, his marriage,
with his birth and death, were all he wished
it to contain. And as the long summer
day faded, the life of this great and good
man went out, and in the words of his
Church's liturgy, he was "gathered to his
fathers, having the testimony of a good
conscience, in the communion of the cath-
olic Church, in the confidence of a certain
faith, in the comfort of a reasonable, relig-
ious and holy hope, in favor with God,
and in perfect charity with the world."

And for what in his life he did for us,
let there be lasting memory. He and the

men of his time have passed away; other
generations have succeeded them; other
phases of our country's growth have come
and gone; other trials, greater a hundred
fold than he or they could possibly have
imagined, have jeoparded the nation's life;
but still that which they wrought remains
to us, secured by the same means, enforced
by the same authority, dearer far for all
that is past, and holding together a great,
a united and a happy people. And all
largely because he whose figure is now
before us has, above and beyond all others,
taught the people of the United States, in
words of absolute authority, what was the
Constitution which they ordained, "in
order to form a more perfect union, establish justice, insure domestic tranquillity,
provide for the common defense, promote
the general welfare, and secure the bless-
ings of liberty to themselves and their
posterity."

Wherefore, with all gratitude, with fitting ceremony and circumstance; in the presence of the highest in the land; in the presence of those who make, of those who execute, and of those who interpret the laws; in the presence of those descendants in whose veins flows MARSHALL's blood, have the Bar and the Congress of the United States here set up this semblance of his living form, in perpetual memory of the honor, the reverence and the love which the people of his country bear to the great Chief Justice.

The ceremonies were concluded with a benediction by the Rev. Dr. J. G. Armstrong.

PROCEEDINGS

OF THE

PHILADELPHIA BAR

IN REFERENCE TO

THE ERECTION

IN

THE CITY OF WASHINGTON

OF A

MONUMENT

TO

CHIEF JUSTICE MARSHALL.

1835—1882.

70

THE BAR OF PHILADELPHIA.

PROCEEDINGS, JULY 7, 1835, ON ANNOUNCEMENT OF THE
DEATH OF CHIEF JUSTICE MARSHALL.

At a meeting of the Bar of Philadelphia, held in the Circuit Court Room July 7, 1835, Mr. P. S. Duponceau was appointed Chairman and the Hon. Charles Smith Secretary. The following resolutions were offered by Mr. John Sergeant and unanimously adopted:

Resolved, That the Bar of the City of Philadelphia participate in the grief which has been caused by the death of the late Chief Justice of the United States, JOHN MARSHALL, and desire to unite with their fellow citizens in expressing their deep-felt respect for the memory of that illustrious man.

Resolved, That while, in common with our fellow citizens, we mourn the great public loss which has been sustained, we feel it to be our privilege as members of a profession so highly honored by the character, talents and services of the deceased, and so long enlightened and directed upon the most momentous topics by his profound and patriotic mind, to be permitted in a special manner to acknowledge our obligations and express our reverence for the name of JOHN MARSHALL: Therefore,

6 M

Resolved, That it be recommended to the Bar of the United States to co-operate in erecting a monument to his memory at some suitable place in the City of Washington.

Resolved, That

Mr. Rawle,	Mr. H. J. Williams,
Mr. Duponceau,	Mr. Kane,
Mr. Sergeant,	Mr. J. M. Read,
Mr. Binney,	Mr. Dunlap,
Mr. Chauncey,	Mr. D. P. Brown,
Mr. C. J. Ingersoll,	Mr. Norris,
Mr. P. A. Browne,	Mr. W. M. Meredith,
Mr. Peters,	Mr. Jas. C. Biddle,
Mr. J. S. Smith,	Mr. Chester,
Mr. J. R. Ingersoll,	Mr. Gilpin,
Mr. Wm. Smith,	Mr. Cadwalader,
Mr. Purdon,	Mr. C. Ingersoll,
Mr. Randall,	Mr. W. T. Smith,
Mr. W. Rawle, Jr.,	Mr. W. B. Reed, and
Mr. Dallas,	Mr. M'Call,

be a committee on the part of the Bar of Philadelphia to unite with their brethren in other parts of the State and Union in carrying the above resolution into effect.

Resolved, That the Bar of Philadelphia will wear crape on the left arm for thirty days, and, if consistent with the arrangements of the near friends of the deceased, will in a body accompany his remains to the place of embarkation for his native State.

Resolved, That Judge Baldwin, Mr. Peters, Mr. Sergeant, Mr. Rawle, jr., Mr. T. I. Wharton, and Mr. E. D. Ingraham be requested, on the part of the Bar, to accompany the remains of Chief Justice Marshall to the City of Richmond, and to attend the funeral there.

Mr. E. C. Ingersoll then offered the following resolution, which was unanimously adopted:

Resolved, That the Chairman and Secretary be a committee to communicate these proceedings and the condolence of the Bar to the family of the deceased.

Mr. Wharton and Mr. Peters moved that Mr. Sergeant be requested to deliver an eulogium upon the character of the late Chief Justice MARSHALL before this Bar at some future time, to be designated by himself.

Resolved, That the preceding resolutions be published in the several newspapers of the city.

MARSHALL MONUMENT.

At a meeting of the committee appointed by the Bar of Philadelphia on the 7th of July, 1835, held at the Law Library Room on the 31st of the same month,

Peter S. Duponceau, Esq., was appointed chairman, and James C. Biddle, Esq., secretary.

The following resolutions were adopted:

Resolved, That Messrs. Duponceau, Sergeant, Binney, Chauncey, and J. R. Ingersoll be a subcommittee whose duty it shall be—

1. To proceed immediately to collect subscriptions for the monument from the Bar of Philadelphia.

2. To cause subscriptions to be collected from the Bar of the other parts of Pennsylvania.

3. To promote subscriptions by the members of the Bar throughout the United States.

4. To correspond with such committees and individuals and members of the profession throughout the United States as may be authorized or disposed to co-operate with us in the proposed object.

5. To confer, on the part of the Bar of Philadelphia, with such committees or individuals as may be appointed or authorized to confer with them, on the subject of their appointment or matters connected therewith.

6. To adopt such other measures as may seem to them expedient and proper for furthering the contemplated purpose.

Resolved, That desiring to make the subscription as extensive as possible, and to avoid inconvenience to those who may be willing to unite with them, it is the wish of the committee that individual subscriptions should be moderate, and that the required amount may be made up by the number of contributors, rather than by the magnitude of particular donations, so that the monument may truly be the work of the Bar of the United States, and an enduring evidence of their veneration for the memory of the illustrious deceased.

Resolved, That it is the desire of the Bar of Philadelphia that all who may contribute may have a voice in selecting the plan to be adopted, and at a suitable time arrangements will be made to give them an opportunity, by their delegates, to take a part in the selection.

Resolved, That before a plan can be adopted it is necessary to know the extent of the means that will be furnished, and therefore it is earnestly requested that subscriptions may be collected and forwarded with the utmost possible dispatch.

Resolved, That Samuel Jaudon, Esq., Cashier of the Bank of the United States, be the Treasurer of the MARSHALL Monument Fund, to whom all moneys collected are to be forwarded.

Resolved, That we sincerely hope that our brethren throughout the United States will immediately and actively exert themselves, within their respective spheres, to collect and forward subscriptions, in such a manner as may seem to them best.

Resolved, That the subcommittee be instructed to receive no subscription from any member of the Bar of Philadelphia exceeding ten dollars, and to inform the members of the Bar throughout the United States that this regulation has been adopted here.

Resolved, That the subcommittee be authorized to add to their number, provided the whole do not exceed nine, and to supply vacancies in their body.

Resolved, That the editors of the newspapers throughout the United States be requested to publish these proceedings.

PETER S. DUPONCEAU,
Chairman.

J. C. BIDDLE,
Secretary.

CIRCULAR

Issued by the Committee of the Bar of Philadelphia shortly after the death of Chief Justice Marshall.

MARSHALL MONUMENT.

PHILADELPHIA, 10*th August,* 1835.

SIR: The subject on which we have the honor of addressing you will, we are confident, require no apology on our part. It needs only to be mentioned to excite in you a feeling responsive to that with which we are impressed.

The death of the late Chief Justice MARSHALL having
taken place in our city, the Bar of Philadelphia lost no time
in assembling in order to deliberate on the honors to be paid
to the memory of the illustrious deceased. Among other
things, it was "*Resolved,* That it be recommended to the Bar
of the United States to co-operate in erecting a monument at
some suitable place in the city of Washington"; and a committee of thirty members was appointed "to unite with their
brethren in other parts of the State and Union to carry that
resolution into effect."

Owing to the indisposition of the chairman of that committee, some delay occurred in calling it together. The same
cause, however, continuing longer than was expected, the committee met on the 31st of last month, and passed the resolutions hereunto annexed, by which you will be informed of
their general views, and of the authority under which we act.

The object of this letter is to solicit your earnest and active
co-operation in this great design. We have reason to believe
that the members of our profession throughout the Union are
in general well disposed towards its execution. We have received offers of co-operation from different States, and from
some of the most distant from us and from each other, as
well by letters addressed to us by committees of the Bars of
particular districts as by the publication of the proceedings
of others in the newspapers. Our hopes of success are
sanguine, and we trust will not be disappointed.

Among the questions which have been asked of us, inquiry
has particularly been made as to what extent and in what
mode it was proposed to raise funds for the contemplated
purpose. As to the extent or amount of the funds to be
raised, you will easily understand that it is a subject on which
we cannot give a positive answer, as it will depend on the
zeal, the activity, and the liberality of our brethren in the

different parts of the United States. When we consider the number of the members of the Bar throughout the Union, and, still more, when we reflect on the strong feeling which they have always evinced for the honor of the profession and the glory of those who have contributed to its illustration, we cannot entertain the least doubt but that a sufficient sum may and will be raised to defray the expense of a monument worthy of ourselves and of the illustrious man whose name and fame it is intended to perpetuate; and in any event we cannot suppose but that enough will be collected for a monument which can never be humble when deriving its splendor from the name to which it will be attached. But it is our earnest wish that it may be such as to reflect honor on the Bar of the United States.

With regard to the mode of collecting funds, we have considered that all the members of our profession are not equally favored with the gifts of fortune; we have had particularly in view the younger members, the hopes of our country, whose zeal and ardor, we know, are not inferior to those of their senior brethren; therefore, in the subscriptions of our own State the general committee thought proper to recommend, and in our immediate district to establish, as far as could be done, a very moderate scale, by limiting the amount of each subscription so as not to exceed ten dollars, although a less sum will not be refused. In doing so, however, we have not meant to exclude individual liberality; it will be in the power of those who can afford and are willing to contribute beyond the amount stated to indulge their generous spirit, either individually or by some concert among themselves, transmitting the amount immediately to the general treasurer, who will be hereinafter mentioned; but the subscription is limited, as we have said, to ten dollars, a sum which we believe there will be but few incapable of contributing.

This is the mode we have adopted for the Bar of our own city and county, leaving to other Bars to adopt such system as they may think proper. We have desired that the money should be paid at the time of subscribing, and so far this, our request, has been complied with. We are happy to inform you that the subscription here is going on in a manner quite commensurate with our expectations.

As soon as we shall have collected a sufficient sum to enable us to form a correct idea of the expense to which we may venture to go for carrying our design into execution, we shall lose no time, with the assent of the general committee, in preparing a suitable plan, and making the contemplated arrangements, to give to the contributors an opportunity, by their delegates, to take part in the selection.

Conceiving it necessary that the money to be raised should be kept together on the same spot, and placed in the hands of a person of acknowledged responsibility, we have thought that we could not do better than to appoint for our treasurer Samuel Jaudon, Esq., the cashier of the Bank of the United States, whose name and character are known throughout the Union. We hope that the moneys collected or otherwise contributed will be transmitted to him as soon as possible.

It may not be improper to add that the designation of those who are invited to contribute is to be understood in the most liberal sense, embracing all who have been of the profession, though now retired, or filling judicial stations, or engaged in other pursuits; nor do we wish to exclude prothonotaries, sheriffs, and other officers intimately connected with the judiciary department, and entitled to be considered as our associates. Should there be any who cannot conveniently subscribe, they may transmit their contributions to the treasurer before mentioned.

Thus, sir, we have stated to you the whole of our views,

and have entered into details as far as we have thought we might do so with propriety. We now earnestly beg that you will use your utmost endeavors, and those of your friends, to promote the great object which is the occasion of this address to you. We hope and wish for the co-operation of every State, Territory and District, and of every county in the Union. Not being acquainted with all the gentlemen whose assistance may be essential, we have to request that you will communicate the substance of this letter, in such manner as you may deem best, to the members of the Bar of your State. If you should have any communications to make to us, please to direct them to William B. Reed, Esq., who acts as secretary to this committee. They shall be respectfully attended to.

We have the honor to be, with great respect, sir, your most obedient, humble servants,

PETER S. DUPONCEAU,
JOHN SERGEANT,
HORACE BINNEY,
CHARLES CHAUNCEY,
J. R. INGERSOLL,
THOMAS DUNLAP,
WILLIAM B. REED,
PETER McCALL,

Committee.

List of subscriptions to the Marshall Monument Fund.

Pennsylvania - - - - - - - - - - - - - -	$1,292
Richmond, Virginia - - - - - - - - -	215
Norfolk, Virginia - - - - - - - - - -	80
New Hampshire - - - - - - - - - -	60
Vermont - - - - - - - - - - - - -	20
Worcester, Massachusetts - - - - - - - -	160
New Haven, Connecticut - - - - - - - -	95
Utica, New York - - - - - - - - - -	100
New York City - - - - - - - - - -	10
Baltimore, Maryland - - - - - - - - -	10
Raleigh and Elizabeth City, North Carolina - - -	130
Charleston, South Carolina - - - - - - - -	180
Augusta, Georgia - - - - - - - - - -	110
Saint Louis, Missouri - - - - - - - - -	95
Total - - - - - - - - - - - - -	2,557

PROCEEDINGS IN 1882.

To the Honorable the Judges of the Court of Common Pleas, No. 2, of the County of Philadelphia:

The petition of the undersigned showeth as follows:

They are the sole survivors of certain members of the Bar of Philadelphia who, in the summer of the year 1835, subscribed certain amounts for the purpose of erecting, at some suitable place in the city of Washington, a monument in memory of JOHN MARSHALL, Chief Justice of the Supreme Court of the United States, who had then just died in this city. The exhibits annexed hereto show particularly the proceedings which then took place, and the list of subscribers to the fund. It did not reach the sum of three thousand dollars, and the amount was entirely inadequate for the purpose desired.

It was, therefore, carefully invested and reinvested in the loan of the city of Philadelphia, at first in the names of "Horace Binney, Joseph R. Ingersoll, William B. Reed, Peter McCall, and Job R. Tyson, trustees of the MARSHALL Memorial Fund," and later in the names of "Horace Binney, William B. Reed, and Peter McCall, surviving trustees of the MARSHALL Memorial Fund." Of these the said Peter McCall was the survivor, and upon his death his executors, John and Richard M. Cadwalader, found among the assets of their testator the said certificates of loan, and cash being interest collected on said loan, the whole amounting in value to about twenty thousand dollars.

At the stated meeting of The Law Association of Philadelphia held on the 5th day of December, 1881, of which a copy of the proceedings is also annexed, a committee was appointed for the purpose of carrying out the objects for which the said fund was subscribed, consisting of

> GEORGE SHARSWOOD,
> WAYNE MACVEAGH,
> JOHN CADWALADER,
> WILLIAM WHITE WILTBANK,
> CHARLES CHAUNCEY BINNEY : as also
> GEORGE W. BIDDLE, Chancellor, and
> WILLIAM HENRY RAWLE, Vice-Chancellor,
> > *Of the Law Association.*

The undersigned show to the Court that they are interested in the proper application of the said fund, and pray the Court to appoint the said committee trustees thereof, and to authorize and empower them to receive the same from the said

executors, or the said city, to give all proper acquittances
and discharges therefor, and to apply the same to the purposes for which it was subscribed.

And they will ever pray, &c.

GEO. SHARSWOOD.
EDWARD OLMSTED.
C. INGERSOLL.
H. CRAMOND.
JOHN L. NEWBOLD.
WILLIAM DUANE.

Decree.

And now, this 28th day of January, A. D. 1882, the within
petition having been read and filed, the Court do grant the
prayer thereof, and do appoint the said George Sharswood,
Wayne MacVeagh, John Cadwalader, William White Wiltbank, Charles Chauncey Binney, George W. Biddle and
William Henry Rawle, Trustees of the said MARSHALL Memorial Fund, without security being required to be given by
them, and do authorize and empower the said Trustees to
receive the same from the executors of Peter McCall, deceased, or the city of Philadelphia, to give all proper acquittances and discharges therefor, and to apply the same to the
purposes for which the said fund was subscribed as appearing
in the exhibits annexed to the said petition, and according to
their true intent and meaning.

And it is further ordered that after said trust shall have
been carried out the said Trustees do make return to this
Court of their action in the premises.

Per Curiam.